Skyscrapers

KATIE MARSICO

Children's Press®
An Imprint of Scholastic Inc.

Content Consultant
Matthew Lammi, PhD
Assistant Professor
Department of Science, Technology,
Engineering, and Mathematics Education
North Carolina State University
Raleigh, North Carolina

Library of Congress Cataloging-in-Publication Data
Marsico, Katie, 1980– author.
Skyscrapers / by Katie Marsico.
 pages cm. — (A true book)
Includes bibliographical references and index.
ISBN 978-0-531-22483-0 (library binding) — ISBN 978-0-531-22273-7 (pbk.)
1. Skyscrapers—Juvenile literature. 2. Skyscrapers—Design and construction—Juvenile literature.
I. Title. II. Series: True book.
NA6230.M37 2016
720.483—dc23   2015022589

© 2016 Scholastic Inc.
All rights reserved. Published in 2016 by Children's Press, an imprint of Scholastic Inc.
Printed in China 62
SCHOLASTIC, CHILDREN'S PRESS, A TRUE BOOK™, and associated logos are trademarks and/or
registered trademarks of Scholastic Inc.
1 2 3 4 5 6 7 8 9 10 R 25 24 23 22 21 20 19 18 17 16

**Front cover: Burj Khalifa tower in Dubai,
United Arab Emirates
Back cover: Lower Manhattan skyline**

Find the Truth!

Everything you are about to read is true *except* for one of the sentences on this page.

Which one is **TRUE**?

T or F The world's tallest skyscraper is in New York City.

T or F Skyscrapers are built to sway slightly in the wind.

Find the answers in this book

Contents

THE **BIG** TRUTH!

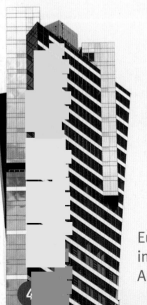

Eureka!

Eureka Tower
in Melbourne,
Australia

4

The Elephant Building in Bangkok, Thailand

The towers of the Bahrain World Trade Center are shaped like sails.

CHAPTER

Dazzling, Dizzying Buildings

Imagine rocketing 1,268 feet (386 meters) above the ground in roughly one minute. That's how long it takes visitors to reach the 102nd floor of One World Trade Center in New York City. After stepping off the elevator, guests are greeted by a dazzling—and sometimes dizzying—360-degree view of the city. This is because they are standing near the top of the tallest skyscraper in the Western **Hemisphere**.

One World Trade Center has observation decks on its 100th, 101st, and 102nd floors.

Malaysia's Petronas Towers are connected by the world's highest double-decker walkway.

Touching the Sky

Skyscrapers are towering **edifices**. They rise high above the skylines of cities and other urban areas. Most modern skyscrapers have a height of at least 656 feet (200 m). With the exception of Antarctica, skyscrapers are found on every continent in the world. These remarkable buildings provide space for people to live and do business without taking up much land.

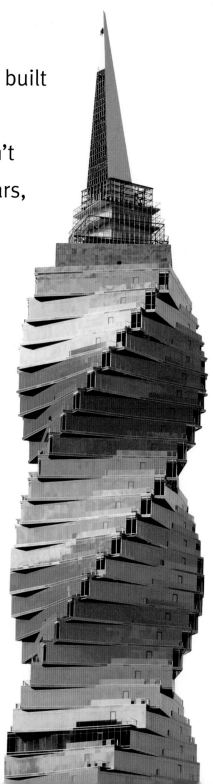

Tall structures have been built for thousands of years. Even so, the term *skyscraper* wasn't used until 1883. Over the years, skyscrapers have become an increasingly major part of most cities. In 2014 alone, work was completed on 97 new skyscrapers. That's approximately quadruple the number built in 2000. It appears likely that even more skyscrapers will dot urban landscapes in the near future.

Panama City, Panama, has a number of skyscrapers, including the spiraled F&F Tower.

The Shard stands among other well-known London landmarks, including Tower Bridge.

Why Skyscrapers Are Significant

Skyscrapers are amazing to behold. Even while serving practical purposes, many skyscrapers also are recognized as landmarks. For example, the Empire State Building and the Chrysler Building are symbols of New York City. Meanwhile, Shanghai, China, is famous for its Shanghai Tower. The Shard is a well-known part of the skyline in London, England.

Skyscrapers are amazing architectural and engineering achievements. These buildings must withstand wind, rain, and other weathering. They must also be able to survive natural disasters such as earthquakes. Building a skyscraper requires careful planning and years of labor. It also needs an artistic vision that stretches far beyond the clouds.

Two workers check blueprints for a skyscraper.

The Great Pyramid at Giza weighs 5.75 million tons.

CHAPTER 2

A Timeline of Tall Buildings

The first "skyscrapers" were built thousands of years ago. They weren't as tall as the Empire State Building or other modern buildings. However, they were still impressive structures for the time. In ancient Egypt, pyramids were the tallest structures. They served as massive burial chambers for early Egyptian rulers called pharaohs. The largest of them was the Great Pyramid at Giza, which dates back to 2575 BCE.

The Great Pyramid and its neighboring pyramids have towered over Giza for thousands of years.

An Ancient Wonder

The Great Pyramid was originally about 480 feet (146 m) tall. Despite its size, workers completed it in less than 20 years. The pyramid was made of limestone blocks. For thousands of years, it was the world's tallest structure. Building anything taller was a challenge in ancient times because of limited engineering technology. In addition, construction materials were very heavy and hard to work with. It was difficult to ensure that brick and stone remained stable at high **elevations**.

Churches Rise High

People constructed more tall buildings during the Middle Ages, which lasted from about 500 to 1500 CE. In many cases, they built elaborate churches that were designed to reach upward toward the heavens. From 1311 to 1548, Lincoln Cathedral in Lincoln, England, was the tallest building in the world. The tip of its central **spire** reached 525 feet (160 m) above the ground.

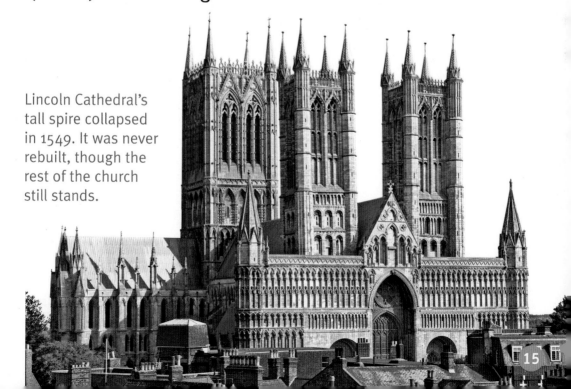

Lincoln Cathedral's tall spire collapsed in 1549. It was never rebuilt, though the rest of the church still stands.

Industrial Advances

In the late 18th and early 19th centuries, the Industrial Revolution took place in nations such as Great Britain and the United States. During this period, a boom in new technology led to rapid growth. People crowded into cities to find work in nearby factories. Architects and engineers responded by designing taller residences to make the most out of the space that was available.

A Timeline of Skyscraper Innovations

1857
The first safety elevators are installed in New York City's E. V. Haughwout Building department store.

1885
The world's first steel-frame building, the Home Insurance Company Building in Chicago, Illinois, opens.

Innovations such as safety elevators and steel frames made it possible to construct taller, sturdier buildings. One of the first U.S. examples was the Home Insurance Company Building in Chicago, Illinois. Completed in 1885, it measured 180 feet (55 m) tall. Soon, architects and engineers started using concrete and glass. With a steel frame and a strong concrete base, or foundation, buildings no longer needed thick outer walls for support. This allowed them to include larger windows.

1931
The Empire State Building becomes the first skyscraper with more than 100 floors.

1895
The Reliance Building in Chicago is the first skyscraper with large windows as most of its outer structure.

1972
The original World Trade Center towers are the first buildings to be taller than the Empire State Building.

A New Design Development

Skyscraper design took a big leap forward in the mid-20th century. Architects and engineers began constructing skyscrapers with several columns of steel or concrete tubes at their center. A series of beams reached outward from these tubes. This design provided greater support and stability.

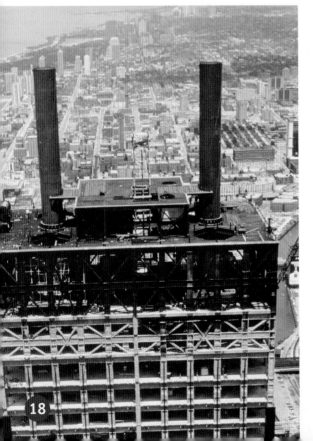

Better stability led to more windows. Many skyscrapers had glass curtain walls, or outer walls made up almost entirely of windows.

Chicago's Willis Tower was the first skyscraper to feature columns of steel or concrete tubes, called bundled tubes, in its structure.

Window Washers

As skyscrapers evolved in cities, so did the window-washing industry. Though this job involves working outside at great heights, it is not as dangerous as it looks. Most window washers who care for skyscrapers work on **scaffolding** or in a special seat that is suspended from a rope. They usually train alongside more experienced washers. This allows them to learn skills such as **rappelling**. These workers also exercise caution by wearing safety harnesses and regularly checking their equipment.

The Transamerica Pyramid is a famous part of the skyline in San Francisco, California.

CHAPTER 3

Creating Safe Structures

In the 21st century, architects and engineers compete to build even higher into the sky. However, height is not their only consideration. Safety is one concern, both during construction and during the building's use. People are constantly searching for new ways to create buildings that can withstand everything from powerful winds to earthquakes.

Architects designed the Transamerica Pyramid to block as little light as possible.

Workers install large windows that will enclose a new building's elevators.

Construction Basics

The amount of time it takes to build a skyscraper varies. In some cases, people have raised 30-story towers in less than a month. In others, construction lasts several years. No matter how long it takes, erecting a skyscraper typically involves a team of many different specialists. These men and women include architects, engineers, interior designers, real estate agents, plumbers, electricians, and elevator consultants.

The Right Stuff

Concrete and steel are two of the main materials used in skyscraper construction. Depending on how the architect wants the skyscraper to look, glass, aluminum, granite, marble, and limestone might form the outer parts of a building. Rubber or plastic is often used to waterproof the roof. When complete, skyscrapers include components such as pipes and electrical and telephone wires. They also have elevators, **ventilation** and sprinkler systems, and other mechanical features.

The five Etihad Towers in Abu Dhabi, United Arab Emirates, took five years to build.

Made to Move

Wind is one of the most important factors when constructing a skyscraper. The taller something is, the greater the effect wind forces have on it. A skyscraper wouldn't be safe if wind gusts, often traveling 100 miles per hour (161 kilometers per hour), whipped its top floors from side to side. If the building was completely stiff, however, the winds would create tremendous pressure.

The skyscrapers in Hong Kong must be able to weather strong storms coming in from the sea.

A tree's trunk and branches bend in the wind. Tall buildings must also be able to sway a little.

Imagine a tree: Dead, brittle branches that do not bend often break off in the wind. Healthy branches, though, sway in the wind and don't break. The same is true for tall buildings. They must sway a little bit. Such motion relieves the pressure wind creates. To make this possible, skyscrapers have joints at the corners of their steel beams. These joints expand and **contract** to allow for slight movement near the tops of the buildings.

Areas such as San Francisco, California, are prone to major earthquakes. Architects have had to find ways to adapt.

Protection From Earthquakes

Sometimes such joints also support a small amount of motion near a skyscraper's foundation. This is especially useful in areas where earthquakes are likely to occur. Despite the shaking ground near its base, a skyscraper needs to remain upright. By enabling the building's foundation to move slightly, joints help ease the overall impact of the shaking.

Dealing With Destructive Glare

Architects and engineers face challenges from the glare of the sun as it reflects off a skyscraper's many windows. Sometimes this glare is so intense that it is capable of melting the paneling and side mirrors of cars that are parked nearby! Fortunately, scientists have created special coatings and films that can be applied to glass to reduce glare.

Light bounces off the windows of the Burj Khalifa in Dubai, United Arab Emirates.

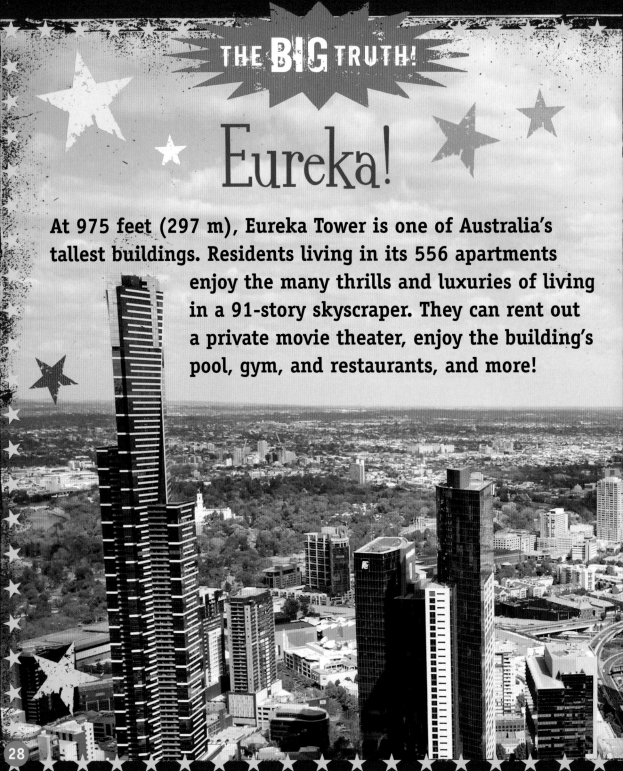

THE BIG TRUTH!

Eureka!

At 975 feet (297 m), Eureka Tower is one of Australia's tallest buildings. Residents living in its 556 apartments enjoy the many thrills and luxuries of living in a 91-story skyscraper. They can rent out a private movie theater, enjoy the building's pool, gym, and restaurants, and more!

The Price of a Penthouse

A luxury apartment near the top of the building was recently priced at $22 million! Potential buyers would be purchasing five bedrooms, five bathrooms, and a 360-degree view of Melbourne.

Going Up?

People going to the top of Eureka Tower can take a 40-second elevator ride. The elevators rocket up at 30 feet (9 m) per second. Alternately, someone going to the observation decks (pictured) can always climb the stairs—all 3,680 of them!

What About the Wind?

The top of Eureka Tower is designed to move almost 24 inches (60 centimeters) on windy days. During periods of extreme wind, residents must keep their balcony doors and windows closed. Leaving them open could create suction. If this occurs, lightweight items such as paper and tablecloths can blow out of apartments.

Incredible Edifices

At present, the Burj Khalifa in the United Arab Emirates is the tallest skyscraper in the world. Construction was completed on it in early 2010. Located in the city of Dubai, the Burj Khalifa has a height of nearly 2,717 ft (828 m). It features 163 floors, 57 elevators, and 8 escalators. It includes private residences, offices, a restaurant, and a hotel.

The Burj Khalifa can be seen 59 miles (95 km) away.

The Asian elephant is Thailand's national animal.

The Elephant Building closely resembles its namesake, the elephant.

From Elephants to Insect Cocoons

In the world of skyscrapers, there is always an even taller building just around the corner. Engineers and architects are forever trying to break the latest height record. However, there are many other remarkable features that can make skyscrapers unique. For example, the Elephant Building in Bangkok, Thailand, is famous for its appearance. The three towers that form this skyscraper resemble the shape of an elephant.

Meanwhile, the Mode Gakuen Cocoon Tower in Tokyo, Japan, looks similar to a cocoon. This skyscraper is primarily an educational building. The people who designed it say its shape is no accident. Architects have stated that, just as young insects mature within a cocoon, students inside the tower prepare to enter Japan's workforce.

Three different schools use classrooms located in the Mode Gakuen Cocoon Tower.

Illuminated Landmark

The Torre Agbar in Barcelona, Spain, isn't famous for its height. It is just 474 feet (144 m) high. However, its front side is equipped with 4,500 yellow, blue, pink, and red lights. At night, the building illuminates Barcelona and is one of the city's most recognizable landmarks.

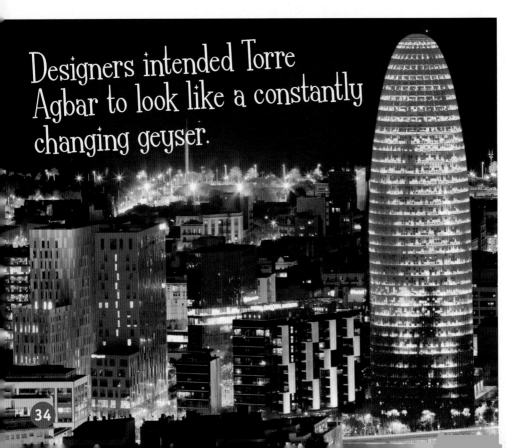

Designers intended Torre Agbar to look like a constantly changing geyser.

The Torre Agbar is now a Hyatt Hotel.

One World Trade Center stands by the National September 11 Memorial.

Buildings That Serve as Symbols

Skyscrapers serve as important symbols of the past, present, *and* future. A well-known example is One World Trade Center (WTC). WTC opened in October 2014. At a height of 1,776 feet (541 m), it ranks among the tallest buildings in the world. It is also famous because it's a reminder of the skyscrapers it replaced. Originally, two buildings known as the Twin Towers stood in WTC's place.

The Twin Towers were a well-known part of New York City's skyline.

On September 11, 2001, terrorists crashed two planes into the Twin Towers. The buildings were destroyed, and 2,753 people died there. In 2006, construction began on a new building to replace the towers. Originally called the Freedom Tower, the name officially changed to One World Trade Center in 2009. It will never erase what happened in 2001. At the same time, the new skyscraper is a symbol of people's ability to remember, rebuild, and look ahead toward the future.

Ghostscrapers

Not all skyscrapers stand along a skyline forever. Some are never even finished. These "ghostscrapers" often face an uncertain fate. Financial problems typically halt their construction or use. As time passes, they fall into disrepair. Here are five of the world's most famous ghostscrapers:

Name of Skyscraper	Location	Height	Date Completed	Date Abandoned	Original Use	Future
The Book Tower	Detroit, Michigan	475 feet (145 m)	1926	2009	Offices, shops, and galleries	Uncertain/ Possible renovation for office space, shops, and residences
The Centro Financiero Confinanzas/ The Tower of David (pictured)	Caracas, Venezuela	620 feet (189 m)	Incomplete	1994	Intended for office space	Uncertain
The Ryugyong Hotel	Pyongyang, North Korea	1,083 feet (330 m)	Incomplete	2012	Intended for a luxury hotel	Uncertain/ Possible completion for use as a hotel
The Sathorn Unique	Bangkok, Thailand	607 feet (185 m)	Incomplete	1997	Intended for residences and shops	Uncertain
The Sterick Building	Memphis, Tennessee	365 feet (111 m)	1930	1986	Offices, shops, and a restaurant	Uncertain/ Possible renovation

Skyscrapers on the Horizon

The future of skyscrapers seems limitless. It's clear that architects and engineers will continue to build higher and higher. Plans are currently in the works to create a tower that will rise 564 feet (172 m) taller than the Burj Khalifa. Construction on Kingdom Tower in Jeddah, Saudi Arabia, will be completed in 2018. When finished, the skyscraper will reach 3,281 feet (1,000 m) into the clouds.

 Kingdom Tower will feature 167 aboveground floors.

Going Greener

The future will inevitably feature taller skyscrapers. It will probably also include greener—or more environmentally friendly— ones. Given their size, skyscrapers often require a great deal of electricity to operate. However, certain fuels used to produce electricity pollute the environment. As a result, many architects and engineers search for alternate ways of meeting skyscrapers' enormous energy needs.

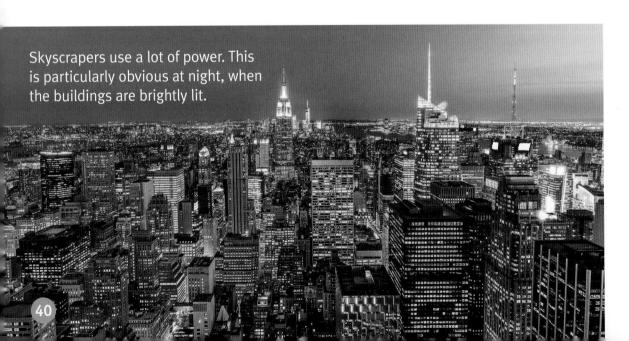

Skyscrapers use a lot of power. This is particularly obvious at night, when the buildings are brightly lit.

The wind turbines on the Bahrain World Trade Center were designed to provide up to 15 percent of the building's power.

One way architects and engineers go green is by designing skyscrapers with built-in wind **turbines**. These machines use wind power to generate electricity. In addition, some skyscrapers include windows that maximize sunlight. This creates a more natural source of heat and light, cutting down on electrical needs. Finally, people are increasing efforts to construct skyscrapers using recyclable materials.

Architects have already started designing possible "farmscrapers."

Future Farms?

Some architects are planning ways to use skyscrapers in food production in the years ahead. Their idea is to grow crops inside extremely tall buildings. People who support this plan say it will help conserve farmland. They also suggest that it will protect crops from the damaging effects of floods and droughts.

Forever Reaching Upward

Farms and turbines are just the beginning. As skyscrapers continue to stretch toward new heights, designs for cleaner, greener buildings will change and grow. Looking forward, who knows what creative thinkers will design next? The ambitions of skyscraper designers are much like the engineering wonders themselves—forever reaching upward. ★

Some buildings include special observation boxes where visitors can see straight down.

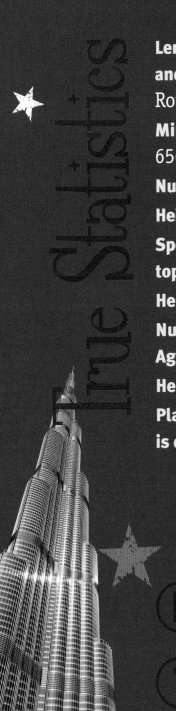

Length of the elevator ride between the ground floor and the 102nd floor of One World Trade Center (WTC): Roughly 1 minute

Minimum height of most modern skyscrapers: 656 ft. (200 m)

Number of new skyscrapers completed in 2014: 97

Height of the Great Pyramid: About 480 ft. (146 m)

Speed of wind gusts that sometimes blow near the tops of skyscrapers: 100 mph (161 kph)

Height of the Burj Khalifa: 2,717 ft. (828 m)

Number of lights that adorn the facade of the Torre Agbar: 4,500

Height of One WTC: 1,776 ft. (541 m)

Planned height of Kingdom Tower when construction is completed in 2018: 3,281 ft. (1,000 m)

Did you find the truth?

F The world's tallest skyscraper is in New York City.

T Skyscrapers are built to sway slightly in the wind.

Resources

Books

Cornille, Didier. *Who Built That? Skyscrapers: An Introduction to Skyscrapers and Their Architects*. New York: Princeton Architectural Press, 2014.

Dillon, Patrick. *The Story of Buildings: From the Pyramids to the Sydney Opera House and Beyond*. Somerville, MA: Candlewick Press, 2014.

Mullenbach, Cheryl. *The Industrial Revolution for Kids: The People and Technology That Changed the World*. Chicago: Chicago Review Press, 2014.

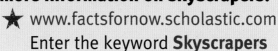

Visit this Scholastic Web site for more information on skyscrapers:
★ www.factsfornow.scholastic.com
Enter the keyword **Skyscrapers**

Important Words

contract (kuhn-TRAKT) — to become smaller

edifices (ED-uh-fiss-iz) — large and usually impressive buildings

elevations (el-uh-VAY-shuhnz) — heights above sea level

hemisphere (HEM-uh-sfeer) — one half of a round object, especially of Earth

innovations (in-uh-VAY-shunz) — new ideas or methods

rappelling (ruh-PEL-ing) — moving down a steep surface by pressing one's feet against it and sliding down a rope

scaffolding (SKAF-uhl-ding) — temporary structures made of planks and poles that workers stand on and that are attached to the outside of a building

spire (SPIRE) — a structure that comes to a point at the top

turbines (TUR-buhnz) — engines powered by water, steam, wind, or gas passing through the blades of a wheel and making it spin

ventilation (ven-tuh-LAY-shuhn) — the process of allowing fresh air into a place and letting stale air out

Index

Page numbers in **bold** indicate illustrations.

About the Author

Katie Marsico graduated from Northwestern University and worked as an editor in reference publishing before she began writing in 2006. Since that time, she has published more than 200 titles for children and young adults. Ms. Marsico has visited Willis Tower in Chicago and would love to one day tour the Empire State Building.